What Comes after This Life?

Crucial Questions booklets provide a quick introduction to definitive Christian truths. This expanding collection includes titles such as:

Who Is Jesus?

Can I Trust the Bible?

Does Prayer Change Things?

Can I Know God's Will?

How Should I Live in This World?

What Does It Mean to Be Born Again?

Can I Be Sure I'm Saved?

What Is Faith?

What Can I Do with My Guilt?

What Is the Trinity?

TO BROWSE THE REST OF THE SERIES,
PLEASE VISIT: LIGONIER.ORG/CQ

CQ

What Comes after This Life?

R.C. SPROUL

 LIGONIER MINISTRIES

What Comes after This Life?
© 2023 by the R.C. Sproul Trust

Published by Ligonier Ministries
421 Ligonier Court, Sanford, FL 32771
Ligonier.org

Printed in China
RR Donnelley
0001122
First edition

ISBN 978-1-64289-440-0 (Paperback)
ISBN 978-1-64289-441-7 (ePub)
ISBN 978-1-64289-442-4 (Kindle)

Cover design: Ligonier Creative
Interior typeset: Katherine Lloyd, The DESK

Ligonier Ministries edited and adapted Dr. R.C. Sproul's original material to create this volume. We are thankful to Mrs. Vesta Sproul for her invaluable help on this project.

Scripture quotations are from the ESV® Bible (The Holy Bible, English Standard Version®), copyright © 2001 by Crossway, a publishing ministry of Good News Publishers. Used by permission. All rights reserved.

Library of Congress Control Number: 2022930809

Contents

Chapter One

Fear and Uncertainty

Death is the greatest problem human beings encounter. We may try to tuck thoughts of it away in the far corners of our minds, but we cannot completely erase our awareness of our mortality. We know that the specter of death awaits us.

The Apostle Paul writes: "Therefore, just as sin came into the world through one man, and death through sin, and so death spread to all men because all sinned—for sin indeed was in the world before the law was given, but sin is not counted where there is no law. Yet death reigned from Adam to Moses" (Rom. 5:12–14). We see that there was sin even before the law was given through Moses, and this is proven by the fact that death occurred before the law was given. The fact of death proves the presence of sin, and the fact of sin proves the presence of law, which has been revealed inwardly to human beings from the beginning. Death came into the world as a direct result of sin.

The secular world views death as part of the natural order, whereas the Christian sees death as part of the fallen order; it was not the original state of man. Death came as God's judgment for sin. From the beginning, all sin was a capital offense. God said to Adam and Eve, "You may surely eat of every tree of the garden, but of the tree of the knowledge of good and evil you shall not eat, for in the day that you eat of it you shall surely die" (Gen. 2:16–17). The death God warned about was not only spiritual but also physical death. Adam and Eve did not die physically the day they sinned; God granted them grace to live for some time longer before exacting the penalty. Nevertheless, they eventually perished from the earth.

Every human being is a sinner and therefore has been sentenced to death. We are all waiting for the sentence to be carried out. The question then is what happens *after* death. For Christians, the penalty has been paid by Christ. This has implications for how we approach death. Paul was in prison when he wrote:

> I know that through your prayers and the help of the Spirit of Jesus Christ this will turn out for my deliverance, as it is my eager expectation and hope that I will not be at all ashamed, but that with full courage now as always Christ will be honored in my body, whether by life or by death. For to me to live is Christ, and to die is gain. If I am to live in the flesh, that means fruitful labor for me. Yet which I shall choose I cannot tell. I am hard pressed between the two. My desire is to depart and be with Christ, for that is far better. But to remain in the flesh is more necessary on your account. (Phil. 1:19–24)

Many of us are staggered by Paul's words in this text. Although we rejoice in Christ's victory over the grave, we nevertheless fear death. Christians are not guaranteed exemption from a painful death. Nevertheless, the thought of death often brings fear for Christians and non-Christians alike. That fear is bound up with the question of what happens after death.

For the Christian, there is a promise from God, a promise that allowed Paul to say, "For to me to live is Christ, and to die is gain." We are promised that we will enter the presence of God. But there are questions, even with this promise. What does heaven look like? Will we enjoy it? What will we do there? What will we be like?

For all the difficulties of this life, it is all we know. After all, even Paul did not denigrate this life. He said: "I am hard pressed between the two. My desire is to depart and be with Christ, for that is far better. But to remain in the flesh is more necessary on your account." Paul desired to continue his life on earth and especially his ministry, but he acknowledged that "to depart and be with Christ" is "far better."

For non-Christians, the news is much less good. There is again a promise from God, but this time it is a promise of punishment, that God's wrath against sin will be satisfied in those who do not trust in Christ. That punishment will happen in a place called hell, but again, there is uncertainty. What is hell like? What does the punishment involve? Is there any chance of escape from it? Is it just, or would it be more just for the wicked to simply be destroyed?

These are important questions, for we will all face death one day. In this booklet, we will examine the biblical data on heaven and hell and seek to dispel the uncertainty we feel. Being consistent Christians means affirming the unflinching supernaturalism of the Bible, a supernaturalism that is anathema to the world today. We must have our worldview shaped by the Bible rather than by the unbelieving culture. As we do so, we will find hope—hope in the God who made us and who promises to bring us to heaven by the work of His Son and to spare us the pains of hell.

Chapter Two

Thinking of Home

What is heaven like? Is there anyone who hasn't raised that question at one time or another? We could first ask, "Is there really such a thing as heaven?" Christianity has been loudly criticized for being a so-called pie-in-the-sky religion. Karl Marx popularized the idea that religion is the opiate of the people. His thesis was that religion had been invented and used by the ruling classes to exploit and oppress the poor people of the world. Religion, Marx claimed, would keep them from revolting by promising them great rewards if they would obey their masters, accept low wages, and so on—but their rewards would be deferred into eternity. In the meantime, these ruthless exploiters of the poor would amass fortunes for themselves here on earth. Marx took the cynical view that religion, with its hope of heaven, has been used as a club to keep unthinking people in line. Versions of this view have become so prevalent that now people are considered unsophisticated if they think at all about a future life, unless they're at a funeral home or at a graveside.

One cannot take Christianity seriously without seeing the central importance of the concept of heaven. There really is a "pie in the sky" idea that is integral to the Bible. I'm afraid we've lost our appetite for, or our taste sensitivity toward, those delights that God has stored up for His people in the future.

Christians are sometimes asked to name their favorite chapter in the New Testament. The top two results are 1 Corinthians 13, the great love chapter, and John 14. John 14 is where we'll begin our brief study of heaven.

In this chapter, Jesus is speaking to His disciples in His last great discourse with them in the upper room on the night of the Last Supper. This is the night on which He was betrayed, the night before His execution. He tells them: "Let not your hearts be troubled. Believe in God; believe also in me. In my Father's house are many rooms. If it were not so, would I have told you that I go to prepare a place for you?" (John 14:1–2). Jesus begins with an admonition to His disciples not to allow their hearts to be distressed or disturbed. This is a call to trust and to faith. These words are so comforting to us that we can sometimes gloss over the cogency of the argument contained in this brief exercise in reason.

Jesus says, "Let not your hearts be troubled," and then He urges them, "Believe in God; believe also in me." Belief in God and belief in Christ are inextricably tied together, for this reason: according to the testimony of the New Testament, it is God who certifies and verifies the identity of Jesus. By endowing Christ with miraculous power and by raising Him from the dead, God proves and certifies that Christ is His beloved Son. Three times the New Testament records that God spoke audibly from heaven, and on all three occasions the announcement that came audibly from heaven was substantially the same thing: "This is my beloved Son." In one case, the voice says "with whom I am well pleased" (Matt. 3:17). Another time it says, "Listen to him" (17:5). In John 14, Jesus is saying that God the Father sent Him into the world, and God the Father bears witness to His identity in the world.

It's in this context that Jesus makes His statements about heaven. Before He makes His announcement about heaven, He speaks of faith in God and faith in Himself. Why does He begin by saying, "Believe in God"? In a real sense, one's relation to God is the controlling idea for one's whole understanding of life, of the world, of death, and of heaven. If there is no God, then there is no reason to have any significant hope for the continuity of personal existence that we call *life*. And yet if God exists, what would be more ridiculous than to assume that He creates creatures in His own image that are ultimately destined for annihilation—to fall into the abyss of nonexistence, to live as grass for a season, only to perish with all our memories, hopes, and labor ending in meaninglessness?

In *Macbeth*, Shakespeare writes about the poor player who "struts his hour upon the stage and then is heard no more." And what's the assessment? "It is a tale told by an idiot, full of sound and fury, signifying nothing." What an image. Here's a person who was in the limelight for a brief interlude of his life, and then suddenly there is only silence. The idea is that if this is the final conclusion to human existence, then the story of life is the idiot's tale. An idiot is someone who is irrational. An idiot is someone who doesn't make sense. He is on the rim of madness, and the tales he tells are not credible stories. They may be filled with sound and fury, noise and passion, but they signify nothing. I think this is the great existential question that every human being faces when he or she faces death.

I'll never forget the day my son arrived. When you see a newborn human who has come into your life, your life changes automatically. All relationships will now be different forever. I remember that occasion vividly because I left the hospital and picked up my mother to take her to see her grandson that evening. When she saw him, she was ecstatic. Later that evening as we walked into her living room, she said, "This is the happiest day of my life." Then we said goodnight.

The next morning, my daughter's yelling awakened me. She came into my room and said, "Grandma won't wake up." As soon as I walked into my mother's room, I realized that she had died in her sleep. When I touched her, her body was cold. It was one of those uncanny moments of human experience. I stood there by her bed, and it seemed to me that just moments before, I had heard my mother say, "This is the happiest day of my life." She had been a living, breathing, caring, passionate, human being, and now she was lifeless. The previous morning, I had seen the newness of life with the birth of my son, and virtually on the same day that my son was born, my mother died. I experienced this conflict between life and death. I stood there and said: "This doesn't make sense. Death doesn't make sense." And every fiber in my being said to me, "This cannot be the final conclusion for human experience."

Now, all of that could be explained by an emotional need in my soul to believe that life is meaningful, but I was thinking in these terms: if God exists, then this cannot be the end. That's what Jesus is telling His disciples when He says, "Let not your hearts be troubled." When I stood beside my mother in that room, my heart was deeply troubled, but Jesus urges: "Don't allow that. Let not your heart be troubled. Believe in God; believe also in Me."

Immediately upon making this connection between faith in the Father and faith in Christ, He states: "In my Father's house are many rooms. If it were not so, would I have told you that I go to prepare a place for you?" (John 14:2). Do you hear what Jesus is saying to His disciples?

As He approaches the moment of His death, He declares to them: "Trust Me. Trust the Father. There is plenty of room in My Father's house, and I am going ahead of you to prepare a place for you." Keep in mind that if Jesus Christ is God incarnate, He's the greatest theologian who ever walked the planet. He doesn't make theological mistakes or approve of theological error. He was not going to allow His disciples to go through the rest of their lives holding to a false belief.

He continues, "And if I go and prepare a place for you, I will come again and will take you to myself, that where I am you may be also" (John 14:3). Jesus says: "I'm going home. I'm going to My Father's house. I'm going to receive My final inheritance, but I'm not going to be alone in heaven. I am going there to prepare a place for you and then I'm coming back, so that where I am, you may be also."

Every single person, Christian or not, longs to be reunited with loved ones who have died, but the Christian longs to be with Christ. I can't wait to see my father, my mother, and my friends in heaven, but beyond that, the ultimate hope of my soul is to see the resurrected Christ in His Father's house, and He promised that this will happen.

Sometimes we shrink in terror and doubt when we contemplate something as wonderful as heaven purports to be. We are sometimes assaulted by the idea that it's just too good to be true, so we're better off living for the here and now. Many people then cling to life in this world desperately, fearful that what lies beyond is worse, but for those who are going to heaven, the bliss that God has stored up for us is unworthy to be compared with any joy or delight we cling to in this life.

Chapter Three

Sitting
on a Suitcase

I think every person who has been married has some kind of humorous story to tell about the honeymoon, and I have one too. It wasn't funny to me at the time because my wife and I had dated for eight years and patiently awaited the day of our wedding, which happened on the afternoon of June 11, 1960, in Pittsburgh. After the wedding came the reception, and after that came another reception at a relative's home, and then after that a long drive to the airport. We finally boarded a flight for JFK Airport in New

York City, where we were going to spend the night at a hotel and fly out the next morning for Bermuda, the destination of our honeymoon.

Before you go on your honeymoon, you look at the pictures in the brochures, and you get some view of the enchantment that awaits you. I could think of no more enchanting place in all the world than Bermuda, and we were very excited about our trip.

Our first problem was that we didn't land at JFK Airport; we landed at Newark Airport. But our hotel was at JFK Airport because we were going to fly from there in the morning. We landed on a Saturday night, and the traffic was horrendous. I asked a cab driver at the airport in Newark how long it would take to get to JFK. When he replied that it would take more than an hour, I said, "No way am I going to do that." So I went back into the airport, and I hired a private plane, a little three-passenger type of thing, to fly us from Newark to JFK. That was an adventure because the plane flew low over the skyline of New York. And in just a few moments, we arrived at JFK.

The next thing was to get from the airport terminal to the hotel. The pilot of this little plane told us to just go inside the terminal building, find one of the courtesy phones on the wall, and call the hotel where we were staying. They would send a limousine to pick us up. So that's what we did. I went over to the courtesy phone and called the hotel. "Yes, we have your reservation, Mr. Sproul. We'll be right over to pick you up." So Vesta and I went to the front of the terminal and sat down on our suitcases to wait. There we sat for an hour and a half on our wedding night, waiting for a limousine that never came. It took me that long to realize that they had forgotten us before I went and called back; they had picked up somebody else, thinking it was us. And we had sat there on our suitcases on our wedding night for an hour and a half.

Here's my question. What would you think of us if I had said, "We're having so much fun sitting here on our suitcases that I think we'll forget about our trip to Bermuda and cancel it"? You would think I had lost my mind. Yet that is the way we behave all the time with respect to heaven. Jonathan Edwards once said that no person who seeks to go on a pilgrimage to a glorious and exotic place will take up permanent residence at an inn along the way. It's nice to have a resting place when we travel, but we're always moving toward that which is better. He said that Christians who cling tenaciously to this world are like sojourners who get stuck in a wayside inn and lose sight of their glorious destination. We are headed for someplace far more glorious than Bermuda. We're headed for heaven. We need to understand not only that there is such a heaven but that this heavenly place is vastly superior to anything we experience in this world.

Let's look at Paul's letter to the Philippian church. Keep in mind that Paul is nearing the end of his life and is now shut up in prison. He's struggling with the circumstances in which he finds himself and makes this statement: "I know that through your prayers and the help of the Spirit of Jesus Christ this will turn out for my deliverance, as it is my eager expectation and hope that I will not be at all ashamed, but that with full courage now as always Christ will be honored in my body, whether by life or by death" (Phil. 1:19–20). Do you hear what Paul is saying? "I don't know what they're going to do with me. They may hack my body to pieces. They may chop off my head. But whether I live or die, Christ is going to be magnified and honored in my body, and I can say that with boldness." How could he face this kind of circumstance with such confidence and serenity of heart and spirit?

The Apostle goes on: "For to me to live is Christ" (v. 21). Paul had one idea, one consuming passion: Christ.

He was so focused on Christ that he said, "For to me to live is Christ." But what's the next part of the statement? "And to die is gain." *Gain* is an antonym for *loss*. We have a tendency to look at death as not only a loss but the worst of all possible losses. Now, it is a loss for us when we lose loved ones to death, but is it necessarily a loss for them? Not if they're destined for heaven.

Paul then writes: "If I am to live in the flesh, that means fruitful labor for me. Yet which I shall choose I cannot tell. I am hard pressed between the two. My desire is to depart and be with Christ, for that is far better. But to remain in the flesh is more necessary on your account. Convinced of this, I know that I will remain and continue with you all, for your progress and joy in the faith, so that in me you may have ample cause to glory in Christ Jesus, because of my coming to you again" (vv. 22–26). From the record of history, it seems that Paul did survive this period of incarceration; this was not his final imprisonment. His earthly ministry was extended so that he could fulfill this idea that he announced to the Philippians.

Do you see the dilemma he expresses? He has experienced a profound sense of ambivalence, a struggle in his heart in terms of his desires. On the one hand, he sees that it's pressingly urgent for the sake of his children in the faith for him to continue to live, and he wants to be of service to them. On the other hand, he desires to depart and be with Christ. And then he gives a little parenthetical statement: "For that is far better." To live is Christ; to die is gain. Paul doesn't say that the difference here is between the good and the better or between the good and the best, but it's the difference between the good and the far better. The best is still beyond heaven, with the final consummation, the resurrection of the body. Even in the state we enter at our death, the Apostle's evaluation is that not only is it a better situation than anything we enjoy in this world, but it is *far* better. What would it do to our lives, our confidence, and the health of our souls if we really believed that?

Some years ago, I was preparing to make a trip to speak at a conference. Everything was scheduled. People had registered for the conference, and there was no way I could arbitrarily cancel my appearance at that conference. The night before I was to leave, I received a phone call that informed me that my beloved mentor, Dr. John Gerstner, had collapsed in Pittsburgh while delivering a series of messages and that he was not expected to live. I was shaken to my boots. Dr. Gerstner had had close encounters with death before, and I had anticipated that at some point he would go home. I had often thought about how I would feel when word came to me that my beloved mentor had died. I would feel like a spiritual orphan. I would feel vulnerable. I would feel alone. I would feel threatened to not have his stabilizing influence in my life anymore, just as children feel when their father is taken from them.

I was very concerned in my soul, but my first thought was mundane: Would I be able to rearrange my schedule to get to the funeral in time if he died in the next forty-eight hours? Then I began to think about how costly this would be for my own life and soul to be without my mentor. Then finally, through the grace of God, I began to think of what it would mean for him, and I thought: "Wow! If Dr. Gerstner goes home now, then my guess is that tonight he'll be sitting at a table talking theology with Luther and Calvin and Augustine and Edwards." And I thought, "Oh, what a glorious thing it will be for him when he crosses the threshold and enters the heavenly sanctuary." Now, this man's indefatigable energy would shame all of us. If I have to speak four times in a single day, I am spent and exhausted, and I can't do anything productive for the rest of the day. And yet Dr. Gerstner, at age seventy-five, could stand in front of a camera and deliver twelve consecutive lectures and then say, "Would you like more?" For him to enter into his rest, into the presence of Christ, is not needful for me but is far better for him.

We know the answer to Paul's struggle. Christ said to Paul: "Not yet, Paul. You still have more work to do. The hour will come when you can come home. I've prepared a place for you, but right now your place is back in the ministry, back working on behalf of the people." For a time, Paul had to live as the people of faith in the Old Testament lived. In Hebrews 11, we read the famous roll call of the heroes of faith, the great chapter that talks about the faith of Abraham, Isaac, Jacob, Joseph, and all the rest. These people in antiquity trusted God. And then we read:

> These all died in faith, not having received the things promised, but having seen them and greeted them from afar, and having acknowledged that they were strangers and exiles on the earth. For people who speak thus make it clear that they are seeking a homeland. If they had been thinking of that land from which they had gone out, they would have had opportunity to return. But as it is, they desire

a better country, that is, a heavenly one. Therefore God is not ashamed to be called their God, for he has prepared for them a city. (Heb. 11:13–16)

The saints of the Old Testament looked beyond the grave, even as Job, who in the midst of his torment and suffering declared: "Though he slay me, I will hope in him. . . . For I know that my Redeemer lives, and at the last he will stand upon the earth" (Job 13:15; 19:25). The Old Testament patriarchs did not have the benefit of the historic record of the resurrection of Christ or of being able to study the words of Jesus, as we are able to study them today. The patriarchs had vague, shadowy hopes and the future promises of God. But on the basis of that, they withstood torture and persecution and hatred and pain and suffering unimaginable because they sought a better country, a heavenly country, and they sought a city whose builder and maker is God. They understood that to depart and enter heaven is far better.

The day after I got that phone call about Dr. Gerstner, I received radically different news. He woke up, the damage was minimal, and two days later he went home. Then a few weeks later he resumed his ministry, and we got the same kind of delay that the Apostle Paul had experienced in the New Testament. Dr. Gerstner simply had to wait longer to enter into his rest.

We're told that there's every conceivable heartache and anguish in the vale of tears that we call life. I remember talking with my grandmother when she was eighty-eight years old. A little tear formed in her eye, and she looked at me wistfully and said: "I just don't understand why God won't take me home. I want to go." As Søren Kierkegaard observed, one of the worst pains that we are ever called to endure is to want to die and not be allowed. We're not allowed to take our own lives. Yet to want to die in order to be free from pain is one thing, but to want to pass beyond the veil to see the face of Christ is something else. Have you come to the place in your thinking where you understand that death is not tragic for the Christian but is a triumph because it means crossing the threshold into glory?

Chapter Four

Rising from the Dust

In a sense, it is naive to ask what heaven is like because no pilgrims have gone to that foreign country and come back with a detailed description of what they found. In the early days of exploration in Western society, people would go out in their sailing vessels, discover new lands, and return with glowing reports of the New World. As Hamlet said, no traveler has returned from that undiscovered country. Earlier in his soliloquy, Hamlet expressed ambivalence about life and death: "To be, or not to be, that is the question: Whether 'tis nobler in the mind to suffer the slings and arrows of outrageous fortune, . . . or by opposing end them." What was he contemplating? He was contemplating suicide: "To die, to sleep—to sleep, perchance to dream." Hamlet contemplated the positive side of restfulness, but then he spoke of that unknown, mysterious dimension of what's over there and the possibility that when we die, we go to something worse; indeed, that is the case for those who fall into the jaws of divine judgment with their death. Shakespeare wrote: "Conscience does make cowards of us all. And makes us rather bear those ills we have, than fly to others that we know not of." Some fear the grave because of a guilty conscience, because they don't know whether they're headed to a place of bliss or a place of final punishment.

We don't know precisely what things are like in heaven. People ask questions such as these: "Will I know my parents? Will I know my wife? Will we be recognizable? How old will we be in heaven? Will our bodies be old and stooped? If we died when we were ninety, will we stay aged forever? And what about children?" All these questions assault us as we try to comprehend what heaven will be like.

People particularly want to know what Jesus meant in Matthew 22 when He was asked which of a woman's seven husbands would be her husband at the resurrection. Jesus responded that in heaven there is no marriage or giving in marriage, but that we are like the angels (Matt. 22:23–33). That statement has provoked all kinds of speculation. Some say that in the resurrection of the body, we're going to be sexless, because angels are sexless. But the Bible doesn't say that angels are sexless, and it certainly doesn't say that we will lose our sex in the resurrection. Jesus simply states that there will be no marrying and giving in marriage. This is a disappointment for people who would like to stay married to their spouse forever. Does Jesus mean that death ends the intimacy that is enjoyed by a husband and a wife, that their relationship will be abolished? I don't know. All He says is "They neither marry nor are given in marriage" (v. 30).

That wording is used one other time in the Bible, in the biblical description of the expansion of wickedness that reached its zenith in the days of Noah, when people were doing what was right in their own eyes and filling the world with violence: they were "marrying and giving in marriage" (24:38). The idea may be that the coming of Christ at the end times will be like the situation in the days of Noah. We can understand this verse in a few ways. One is that it may refer to the suddenness of the appearance of divine judgment, when people are going about the normal activities that characterize life as we know it, marrying and giving in marriage. Perhaps all that Jesus means to say is that the suddenness of His appearance will be like that.

Yet there is another theory about Matthew 24:38 that I cannot confirm or prove, but that I find fascinating and interesting. Some say that the phrase "marrying and giving in marriage" was a Jewish idiomatic expression for a low view of the sanctity of marriage in a degenerate culture in which marriage had no sense of permanence. People were getting married and then quickly divorcing, and marrying again, and then marrying still again. This was characteristic of the decadence of the age of Noah, which provoked God to bring the flood. It could be that when Jesus was asked who the man's wife would be in the resurrection, He was essentially saying, "That's not going to be a problem in the resurrection because we're not going to have this cycle, this facile pace of marrying and giving in marriage."

Another possibility is that Jesus was saying that in the resurrection there will no longer be marriage as we know it. That makes us wonder whether the joy that accompanies the relationship of intimacy that God has given us in this world will be over. Here is my purely speculative thought. What if in the resurrection you are so sanctified that you can enjoy an in-depth, intimate, personal relationship with every other inhabitant of heaven that exceeds in intimacy and joy even the most joyous, personal, intimate relationship you had on earth? I think there's sound reason to believe that I will be able to relate as closely, as openly, and as warmly to a thousand women in the resurrection as I do to my wife now. In fact, I'll have a deeper personal relationship with people that I don't even know now than any relationship I enjoy in this world, once sin has been removed, because when we are glorified as human beings, all the barriers to deep, personal relationship and communication that exist because of sin will be gone. Maybe that's the secret that Jesus is hinting at when He says that there will be no marriage or giving in marriage in the resurrection.

The Sadducees who asked Jesus about marriage in the resurrection didn't believe in the resurrection; they were only trying to trap Him (Matt. 22:23). Likewise, today there are many who don't hold to a resurrection, even some who want to retain a kind of Christianity that does not embrace the resurrection. I had a roommate in college who went into the ministry, and I remember the day of his ordination exams. He was going to go before the presbytery to be examined on his doctrine. My friend looked at me and said, in a spirit of panic, "Should I go with the resurrection of Christ or not?" I didn't know what he meant. He asked, "Should I tell the presbytery I believe that Christ was raised from the dead or not?" I said, "Well, what do you believe?" He said, "I don't think He was." I told him that he was morally bound to say that. "If you don't believe in the resurrection of Christ, you can't conceal that from the presbytery," but he did conceal it, and he was ordained. Ironically, a few years later I came before the same presbytery and stood in front of two hundred clergy to be examined, and the main examiner was that same friend. He had to look me in the eye when he asked me whether I believed in the resurrection, and he was afraid I was going to say, "Yes, I do, but do you?" But I wasn't about to put him on trial there.

We recall that one of the most important lines found in the Apostles' Creed is the statement "I believe in . . . the resurrection of the body." That affirmation is not a statement about *Christ's* resurrection. To be sure, the Apostles believed in the resurrection of Christ, but that statement does not refer to the resurrection of Christ's body. It refers to our confidence that *we* will participate in the bodily resurrection of Christ. We're saying that we believe that our bodies will be raised from death and will be perfected, and that we'll be reunited with our souls. That's what it means to say, "I believe in . . . the resurrection of the body."

We muse on these matters and ask all kinds of questions. But we're not the first to ask them. In his letter to the Corinthians, Paul spent a good deal of time talking about the concept of heaven as it related to the resurrection of Christ. In 1 Corinthians 15, Paul gives a marvelous defense of the historical reality of the resurrection of Jesus and demonstrates that His resurrection is central to Christianity and essential to Christian faith.

Paul provides a logical progression when he reasons, "If there is no resurrection, then all kinds of things would follow from it" (see vv. 13–19). After he gives his defense of the truth of Christ's resurrection, Paul then answers another question: "But someone will ask, 'How are the dead raised? With what kind of body do they come?'" (v. 35).

After Paul raises this question, he exclaims: "You foolish person! What you sow does not come to life unless it dies"

(v. 36). Here he borrows a statement almost verbatim from Plato and Socrates, an analogy drawn from nature. You take a seed, and you plant it in the ground. Then you continue to water it and expose it to sunlight. Why do you do that? Because you're trying to see the germination of life. You want that seed to produce a flower or vegetable or grass. You want new life to come forth, and so you water it. Why? So that the water will impart life to the seed? No. What does the water do? It kills the seed. It makes it rot, because the seed has to rot and die, as it were, before the germination takes place—just like the metamorphosis involved in the transformation of the caterpillar to the butterfly. The one has to leave and be changed into the other. And that's what Paul is saying: "What you sow does not come to life unless it dies. And what you sow is not the body that is to be, but a bare kernel" (vv. 36–37). If we want grass, we don't throw grass into the dirt. We throw grass *seed* into the dirt. If you want flowers, you don't take the bloom from the flower and throw it into the ground and water it. You have to take seeds from the flower and put them into the ground and water them. Paul writes that this is a kernel "perhaps of wheat or of some other grain. But God gives it a body as he has chosen, and to each kind of seed its own body" (vv. 37–38).

When I was a child, my mother made me plant a garden. We sent away for little packages of flower and vegetable seeds. She showed me how to plant them in a straight row and how to space them so that there would be room for the mature plant to spread, and so on. After I planted all the seeds, I had to take the packages that the seeds had come in and use Popsicle sticks and make signs out of the seed packages. I stuck the signs into the ground where I had put the seeds. Why was that? So that I would know what kind of seed I had planted where, before the plants emerged. It turns out that I was good at growing seed packages on sticks but not so good at growing flowers.

Paul is pointing out something basic to life. There are all kinds of different bodies in the world, all kinds of different living things, different grains, flowers, and vegetables. They come from different seeds, and different seeds produce different kinds of bodies. Paul says: "Not all flesh is the same, but there is one kind for humans, another for animals, another for birds, and another for fish. There are heavenly bodies and earthly bodies, but the glory of the heavenly is of one kind, and the glory of the earthly is of another. There is one glory of the sun, and another glory of the moon, and another glory of the stars; for star differs from star in glory. So is it with the resurrection of the dead" (vv. 39–42). The Apostle is saying: "Open your eyes to the wide diversity of reality that you experience, all different sizes, shapes, forms, and structures of existing entities in the universe: stars and moons and trees and mountains and grass and waterfalls. If you look just at the animal kingdom, you'll see a myriad diversity of kinds of life."

Do we think that in our experience we have seen every conceivable kind of life and body that there is? In our fantasies and sci-fi movies, the creative imaginations of the screenwriters produce all kinds of robots and creatures and aliens: different kinds of life and different kinds of bodies. And Paul is saying, "There is a kind of body that no one has seen yet." The resurrected Christ came out of the tomb with the same body with which He went into the tomb—His resurrected body had continuity with the one that had been buried. But it also had discontinuity because it had been changed. His was now a glorified body. Paul is pointing out that we are being prepared for a whole new dimension of life and of bodily existence.

He writes: "So is it with the resurrection of the dead. What is sown is perishable; what is raised is imperishable" (v. 42). The body that I have now is getting old; it's getting weak; it's decaying; it's undergoing a loss of strength and vitality. It is corrupting. I long for a new body. Our new body will be incorruptible. It will be invincible. It won't age. It won't decay. It won't wear out. It won't rot. It won't break. It won't get sick.

> It is sown in dishonor; it is raised in glory. It is sown in weakness; it is raised in power. It is sown a natural body; it is raised a spiritual body. If there is a natural body, there is also a spiritual body. Thus it is written, "The first man Adam became a living being"; the last Adam became a life-giving spirit. But it is not the spiritual that is first but the natural, and then the spiritual. The first man was from the earth, a man of dust; the second man is from heaven. As was the man of dust, so also are those who are of the dust, and as is the man of heaven, so also are those who are of heaven. (vv. 43–48)

Paul concludes with this: "Just as we have borne the image of the man of dust, we shall also bear the image of the man of heaven" (v. 49). We will have a body like the body of Christ.

We've asked the question, "In the resurrection, will we be able to recognize people who are there?" Certainly their outward appearances will have changed. We're accustomed to recognizing people strictly on the basis of outward appearances. The whole idea of cognition, of being able to identify certain traits of people, is an incredibly strange thing.

I have an interest in oil painting. I'm a novice at it, but I undertook a project to paint a portrait of Martin Luther, and I had to do it in stages. The first stage is a very rough outline, trying to get the proportion of the head right and get the ear lined up with the nose, and so on, before working on details. One night after roughing in the basic proportions of the portrait of Luther, I cleaned up my paints and stood back, looking at the painting from about thirty feet away. I said, "Vesta, look at that!" She said, "What?" I said, "If I walked in here and somebody else was painting that portrait, and I saw it from here in its raw and unfinished state, I would instantly know it was a portrait of Martin Luther." That's not a testimony to my artistic ability. But something was already there on the canvas, even though it was so incomplete and unlike an exact replica of Martin Luther's face. There was something I could recognize in that and say, "That's Luther."

Jesus' body was different when He came out of the tomb. It was so different that people did not immediately recognize Him, but with a second glance they could sometimes see that it was Jesus. When you see your departed friends and relatives in the resurrection, they will appear different from how they appeared on earth. When you see them, you will know them, and they will know you. We have no reason to worry about that at all.

Chapter Five

No More Tears

Christians often think that heaven will be a place that is somewhat ethereal and spiritual, in some faraway land east of the sun and west of the moon. The expectation is that the world in which we now live will be completely annihilated, and that we will live in some vaporized place in the sky. The New Testament does not teach the final, ultimate destruction of this world; rather, the view of the New Testament is of the renovation of this fallen planet. Paul tells us in Romans, for example, that the whole creation groans together in travail, waiting for the manifestation of the sons of God (Rom. 8:22–23). In the consummation of the kingdom of God, in the final eschatological triumph of Christ, this world may go through a radical purging, but it will not be destroyed. It will be renewed. Heaven will be here after the earth has been transformed. We find this beautiful imagery in the last two chapters of Revelation. There we read of John's vision of the new heaven and of the new earth, and of the heavenly city, the new Jerusalem, that descends from heaven to the earth.

In all of Scripture, the place that gives us the most vivid and graphic description of what heaven is like is the unveiling we find in the book of Revelation. This book is an example of apocalyptic literature, which is known for its heavy use of rich images and symbols, and so it sounds strange to us when we hear the descriptions of streets of gold and gates of pearl and so on. But these images and symbols all point beyond themselves to profoundly important realities.

John writes, "Then I saw a new heaven and a new earth, for the first heaven and the first earth had passed away, and the sea was no more" (Rev. 21:1). I find it striking that the first statement that describes this new heaven and new earth is negative. It speaks of the absence of something, in this case the absence of the ocean. There is no sea. Now, that might come as a tremendous disappointment to those who have sand in their shoes and who are in love with beaches. It might seem that a new heaven and a new earth without the sea would be a paradise without the necessary ingredients. But a Jewish person hearing this description would recognize its symbolic importance. In Hebrew poetry, the sea is the symbol of destruction because in the history of the Jewish people, the sea was not their friend. Israel never developed a commercial sea trade. Rather, the sea was the place from which marauders came. Their archenemies, the Philistines, controlled the seacoast. The seacoast was rocky and treacherous and dangerous, and terrible storms that swept in across the Mediterranean would stir up the lakes and bring the hot winds of the sirocco. All those came off the sea, and so the sea was the image of destruction. In Psalm 46, the sea roars and is troubled, and it beats against the mountains.

The positive image in Hebrew poetry is the river or the spring. The river Jordan, for example, cuts like a ribbon right down the middle of the arid, desert land and is the source of life and nourishment. As we will see, in the new

Jerusalem, a river of life flows right down the center of the city. And so we see the absence of the sea but the presence of the river. The absence of destruction, the absence of danger, and the presence of life are symbolized here.

Then the Apostle writes: "And I saw the holy city, new Jerusalem, coming down out of heaven from God, prepared as a bride adorned for her husband. And I heard a loud voice from the throne saying, 'Behold, the dwelling place of God is with man. He will dwell with them, and they will be his people, and God himself will be with them as their God'" (Rev. 21:2–3). The Greek word translated "dwelling place" is also translated "tabernacle," drawing on the imagery of the Old Testament. God's dwelling among His people was signified by the tabernacle, the tent that was pitched in the center of the camp of the twelve tribes of Israel. The twelve tribes were situated almost like a clock, and in the very center of that clock was the tabernacle, indicating that God was in the midst of His people.

In the prologue to his gospel, John declares, "And the Word became flesh and dwelt among us . . . full of grace and truth" (John 1:14). "And dwelt among us" is a loose translation of the actual language used in the original text. The text literally says, "And the Word became flesh and *tabernacled* among us" or "pitched His tent in our midst," referring back to the symbolic presence of God in the tabernacle of the Old Testament.

John sees this new Jerusalem coming out of heaven, looking like a bride adorned for her husband, and he hears a loud voice from heaven itself make the announcement: "Behold, the dwelling place of God is with man. He will dwell with them, and they will be his people, and God himself will be with them as their God" (Rev. 21:3). What does this vision tell us? God Himself will be with His people. God comes to be in the midst of His people. Nothing is more glorious than to be bathed in the radiance of the unveiled presence of God.

Then we read this: "He will wipe away every tear from their eyes, and death shall be no more, neither shall there be mourning, nor crying, nor pain anymore, for the former things have passed away" (Rev. 21:4). When I was a little boy, I would sometimes get into scrapes. A certain boy in our town was something of a bully. He towered over the rest of us, and he could be somewhat mean. One day he started calling me bad names and making fun of me. He hurt my feelings, and I started to cry and went home. I opened the screen door, and my mother was standing in the kitchen. She was cooking, and she had an apron on. As I was crying, she dropped her spoon and rushed over and grabbed me and hugged me and asked, "What's the matter?" Through my sobs, I told her that this fellow had been treating me in a bad way, and she was very tender. She calmed me down, took the edge of her apron, and dried my tears.

I was visiting a friend in the hospital in Boston many years ago. He was in the final hours of his life, and I can remember being by his hospital bed and feeling utterly helpless. I couldn't do anything to help him except to take little pieces of ice and put them to his lips, which were parched. As I was doing this on one occasion, he looked at me. He was too weak to even speak. A single tear formed in his eye, and I picked up the little cloth that was on the bedstand and wiped away that tear. It is difficult to describe something like that—what is communicated from one human being to another when that kind of service is rendered, the drying of someone's tears.

I found great consolation and comfort when my mother wiped away my tears. My weeping stopped, and I was restored to a sense of equilibrium. But guess what? I cried again and again over the years. John tells us that when

God personally comes to His people and dries their tears, it will be the end of all crying—at least crying from pain or sorrow or grief or unhappiness. There is a permanence in heaven of cessation of these things because, the text tells us, there will be no more death. There will be no more pain. There will be no more sorrow. All the things that provoke us to weep will no longer be present. In fact, one of the most amazing things about this description of the nature of heaven is the emphasis again and again on what is not in heaven. There is no sea. There is no death. There are no tears. There is no sickness. There's no pain. There's no sin. That is not an exhaustive list, but it's interesting to notice that the first thing that is announced, basically, is the end of suffering:

> And he said to me, "It is done! I am the Alpha and the Omega, the beginning and the end. To the thirsty I will give from the spring of the water of life without payment. The one who conquers will have this heritage, and I will be his God and he will be my son. But as for the cowardly, the faithless, the detestable, as for murderers, the sexually immoral, sorcerers, idolaters, and all liars, their portion will

be in the lake that burns with fire and sulfur, which is the second death."

Then came one of the seven angels who had the seven bowls full of the seven last plagues and spoke to me, saying, "Come, I will show you the Bride, the wife of the Lamb." And he carried me away in the Spirit to a great, high mountain, and showed me the holy city Jerusalem coming down out of heaven from God, having the glory of God, its radiance like a most rare jewel, like a jasper, clear as crystal. It had a great, high wall, with twelve gates, and at the gates twelve angels, and on the gates the names of the twelve tribes of the sons of Israel were inscribed—on the east three gates, on the north three gates, on the south three gates, and on the west three gates. And the wall of the city had twelve foundations, and on them were the twelve names of the twelve apostles of the Lamb. (Rev. 21:6–14)

The description goes on to point out several things. First, the new Jerusalem is a city that comes from heaven, and its dimensions form a perfect cube. What does that call to mind? It recapitulates the dimensions of the earthly

Holy of Holies, which was also a perfect cube. Revelation also speaks of the foundations and the walls, and the number twelve figures prominently. The city is inhabited by 144,000, which is simply taking the number twelve and multiplying it by twelve and then taking it to the superlative degree, which in this case is the thousands. This is the perfect number of fullness. The multiples of twelve refer both to the twelve tribes of Israel, who are commemorated in the city, and to the twelve disciples of Christ, who are also part of the foundation of the new Jerusalem. Remember, this is a city whose builder and maker is God, and the city of God rests on the foundation of the Old Testament prophets and the New Testament Apostles, with Christ being the chief cornerstone.

"And the twelve gates were twelve pearls, each of the gates made of a single pearl, and the street of the city was pure gold, like transparent glass" (v. 21). Gorgeous jewels adorn the city (see vv. 18–20), and the twelve gates are twelve pearls. Each individual gate is one pearl. Imagine that. You've heard the reference to the pearly gates. Each gate is a single pearl, brilliant and magnificent. The beauty of the light that floods the city is reflected in these pearls and refracted from the facets of the jewels that adorn the city. The streets of the city are said to made of transparent gold. We don't think of gold as transparent. For gold to be transparent, it has to be rolled out so thin that one can see through it.

We go on and read about some more things that are not there: "And I saw no temple in the city" (v. 22). If there's one place where we would expect a temple, it would be in heaven. It's one thing to say that there will be no death or weeping or sorrow or sickness or sea, but John tells us that there is also no temple. There's no need of a temple in heaven because the temple symbolizes the presence of God with His people. Now, when God is there in reality, present with His people, there will be no need for the earthly representation. "For its temple is the Lord God the Almighty and the Lamb. And the city has no need of sun or moon to shine on it, for the glory of God gives it light, and its lamp is the Lamb" (vv. 22–23). That's another fantastic image: no sun. If there were a sun in heaven, we wouldn't be able to see it in any case. It would be blotted out by the superintensity of the radiance and refulgent glory of God Himself, which is so much more dazzling than any created thing like the sun. There is no sun or moon because they're unnecessary. The illumination of this city comes from the glory of God and of Christ.

And then we read in chapter 22:

Then the angel showed me the river of the water of life, bright as crystal, flowing from the throne of God and of the Lamb through the middle of the street of the city; also, on either side of the river, the tree of life with its twelve kinds of fruit, yielding its fruit each month. The leaves of the tree were for the healing of the nations. No longer will there be anything accursed, but the throne of God and of the Lamb will be in it, and his servants will worship him. They will see his face, and his name will be on their foreheads. And night will be no more. They will need no light of lamp or sun, for the Lord God will be their light, and they will reign forever and ever. (Rev. 22:1–5)

What else is absent from the new Jerusalem? The curse of God. The wrath of God. The judgment of God. And rather than darkness, which indicates the curse, here the ultimate joy of heaven will be in our experience of the beatific vision—the vision of the face of God, uncovered, unhidden, unveiled. We will look directly into the unveiled face of God, for we will see Him as He is.

I'd like you to take the time to read Revelation 21–22 in its entirety, and think of it as a letter from heaven, addressed to you, describing this place where Christ promised to go to prepare a place for you, if indeed you are in Him. We need to keep this vision of the new heaven and new earth in front of us at all times, when death will be completely swallowed up by the victory of the Lamb and of His kingdom. We need to keep that image before our eyes, so that every tear that we shed in this vale of tears is not wasted.

Chapter Six

The Place of God's Disfavor

Having looked at the biblical doctrine of heaven, the resurrection, and the new heaven and new earth, we now turn our attention to the doctrine of hell. I don't suppose there is any topic in Christian theology that is more difficult to deal with than the doctrine of hell. In fact, the doctrine has been so controversial that in the modern era it's almost never referred to. We've turned against the old-fashioned revival preaching that was characterized by the idea of hellfire and brimstone to never mentioning the threats of hell at all.

Perhaps no theologian or preacher is more closely associated with the concept of hell than Jonathan Edwards. In college, my psychology textbook treated Edwards as an illustration of somebody who was sadistic because he seemed to preach so often on the subject of hell. That bothered me at the time, doing psychoanalysis from a distance of a couple of centuries. When people take the time to read Edwards deeply, they discover that Edwards certainly believed in the reality of hell and certainly had a passionate concern for the spiritual well-being of the people in his congregation. If a pastor believed in hell and didn't love his people, he would sadistically do everything in his power to persuade them that there was no such place as hell. The sadistic person gets some kind of delight or glee out of contemplating another person's torment or torture. That was certainly not true of Edwards.

From the vantage point of the twentieth century, we have this allergy against any serious discussion of the doctrine of hell. In fact, in probably no other time in the history of the church have more people challenged the doctrine than in our own day. Liberal theologians completely dismiss it as part of the mythological worldview of primitive people, a concept unworthy of the love of God and the love of Jesus. Others, even within the professing evangelical camp, have created quite a stir by suggesting the doctrine of annihilationism, which says that the ultimate judgment of the sinner is not some kind of ongoing, eternal punishment in a place called hell but simply the annihilation of the person's existence. They believe that the great loss involved in annihilation is the loss of a happiness promised to those who will live eternally in heaven.

The concept of hell was not invented by Jonathan Edwards or by John Wesley or by any of the frontier revival preachers. Nor was it invented by the Reformers of the sixteenth century or by Thomas Aquinas or by Augustine. Almost everything that we learn, biblically, about hell comes to us from the lips of Jesus Himself. It's because Jesus spoke so frequently about hell that the church takes the concept so seriously (or at least should take the concept seriously).

In a lecture series on hell years ago, Dr. John Gerstner said that the whole idea of a hell that involves some kind of eternal punishment at the hands of a just and holy God is so profoundly difficult for us to handle emotionally that the only person with enough authority to convince us of the reality of such a place would be Jesus Himself.

When I discuss the doctrine of hell, people often ask me whether I believe that the New Testament portrait of hell is to be interpreted literally. The New Testament, after all, contains vivid descriptions of hell. It is called a place of torment, a pit, the place of eternal fire, or the abyss (as in Revelation). It is also described as the place of "outer darkness" (Matt. 25:30). So I respond by saying, "No, I don't interpret those images literally." There are several reasons for that, which I'll get into in a moment. When I say that I don't take them literally, however, and instead refer to them as symbols or figures or metaphors or images, people breathe a deep sigh of relief. They exclaim, "Oh, I'm so glad to hear that you don't take them literally."

Let me say a couple of things about taking these images literally. One of the reasons that classical orthodox theology has tended not to take these images in exact literal terms is that if we did, we would have a difficult time making them agree with one another. If the place of hell is a burning fire on the one hand and a place of outer darkness on the other, that's difficult to reconcile because usually where there's fire, there's light. You can't have fire in total darkness. There is a kind of collision of images there.

THE DEAL

HEAVEN OR HELL, WHICH ONE FOR YOU?

God gives every man the following choice: "For the wages of sin is death; but the gift of God is eternal life through Jesus Christ our Lord." (Romans 6:23)

THE NEGATIVE ASPECTS OF THE DEAL

1. The Bible states that you are a sinner. "For there is not a just man upon earth, that doeth good, and sinneth not." (Ecclesiastes 7:20) "As it is written, There is none righteous, no, not one:" (Romans 3:10)

2. The price of sin is to be separated from God and to spend all eternity in hell. "Wherefore, as by one man sin entered into the world, and death by sin; and so death passed upon all men, for that all have sinned:" (Romans 5:12) "And death and hell were cast into the lake of fire. This is the second death. And whosoever was not found written in the book of life was cast into the lake of fire." (Revelation 20:14-15)

THE POSITIVE ASPECTS OF THE DEAL

1. Jesus Christ, the Son of God, has paid the penalty for your sin. "...without shedding of blood is no remission." (Hebrews 9:22) "But God commendeth his love toward us, in that, while we were yet sinners, Christ died for us." (Romans 5:8)

"For the life of the flesh is in the blood: and I have given it to you upon the altar to make an atonement for your souls: for it is the blood that maketh an atonement for the soul." (Leviticus 17:11)

2. Salvation is a gift, and cannot be earned. "For by grace are ye saved through faith; and that not of yourselves: it is the gift of God: Not of works, lest any man should boast." (Ephesians 2:8-9) "Not by works of righteousness which we have done, but according to his mercy he saved us..." (Titus 3:5)

THE TERMS OF THE DEAL

1. "...Sirs, what must I do to be saved? And they said, Believe on the Lord Jesus Christ, and thou shalt be saved..." (Acts 16:30-31) "Neither is there salvation in any other: for there is none other name under heaven given among men, whereby we must be saved." (Acts 4:12). "He that believeth on the Son hath everlasting life: and he that believeth not the Son shall not see life; but the wrath of God abideth on him." (John 3:36).

2. Are you willing to accept God's deal? If you are, admit to God that you are a guilty sinner and that you desire to be delivered from your sinful condition. "...except ye repent, ye shall all likewise perish." (Luke 13:3).

3. God gives you this promise: "That if thou shalt

confess with thy mouth the Lord Jesus, and shalt believe in thine heart that God hath raised him from the dead, thou shalt be saved. For with the heart man believeth unto righteousness; and with the mouth confession is made unto salvation." (Romans 10:9-10)

If you will accept Jesus Christ as your Saviour, please pray this prayer or one similar to it: "Dear Heavenly Father, I know I am a sinner and need your forgiveness. I believe that Jesus died for my sin. I am willing to turn from sin. I now ask Jesus Christ to come into my heart and life as my personal Saviour. I am willing, by God's grace, to follow and obey Christ as the Lord of my heart and life."

If you have decided to trust Jesus Christ as your Saviour after reading this tract, please write and let us know.

Name _____

Address _____

City _____ Zip _____

State _____ Age _____

FELLOWSHIP TRACT LEAGUE
P.O. BOX 164 • LEBANON, OH 45036 • mail@fellowshiptractleague.org
www.fellowshiptractleague.org © Tract 136
All tracts free as the Lord provides. Not to be sold.

Before we breathe too deep a sigh of relief, we must consider something else. If we take the position that hell is described in symbolic language in the New Testament, then we have to ask, What is the function of a symbol? The function of figurative, metaphorical language in Scripture is to demonstrate a likeness to a reality. A symbol is not the reality itself. The symbol points beyond itself to something else. The question arises, Is the reality to which the symbol points less intense or more intense than the symbol? The assumption is that there's always more to the reality than what is pointed to by the symbol. This makes me think that the reality toward which these symbols point is more ghastly than if we were to take the images literally. I heard a theologian say that the sinner in hell would do everything he could and give everything he had to be in a literal lake of fire rather than to be in hell itself. We don't know exactly where hell is or how it operates. But all the imagery that our Lord uses suggests that it is a place where we don't want to go. It is a place of unspeakable pain and torment.

Historically, the question has been whether the pain or the punishment that people endure in hell is physical punishment. The Scriptures speak about the resurrection of the body not only for the believer but also for the unbeliever, and the biblical writers say that ultimately the person in hell, after the last judgment, will be in a resurrected body suited for his punishment. Because so much of the language of hell in the New Testament speaks about corporeal punishment, many have drawn the conclusion that hell does involve a relentless, endless physical kind of suffering.

That may be the case, but other theologians have suggested that the essence of the torment is found in the torment of the soul, of the person whose soul has been cut off from the blessedness of the presence of God and from His grace. To carry around that spiritual distress within a resurrected body would be torment enough. But again, those are issues that we can only speculate about.

Let's look at some of the New Testament passages that speak of this place called hell. In Matthew 25, Jesus tells the parable of the talents, and He says: "For to everyone who has will more be given, and he will have an abundance. But from the one who has not, even what he has will be taken away. And cast the worthless servant into the outer darkness. In that place there will be weeping and gnashing of teeth" (Matt. 25:29–30). Here Jesus uses two images. One is the image of "outer darkness."

People ask me if I think that hell is separation from God. I usually reply, "Yes and no." I say, "Yes, hell is a separation from God." Again, people express relief when I say that. Does that mean simply that hell is a place where God is completely absent, and therefore hell is not necessarily a lake of fire; it's just people gathered in a place? This is the imagery in Jean-Paul Sartre's little play *No Exit*, in which people are confined and condemned to a miserable existence dealing with each other, without the presence of God. But before you feel relief that hell represents the absence of God, let's think about that for a moment.

Our language today contains various allusions and references to hell. You've heard them. Somebody comes back from being in the military and uses the expression "War is hell." Or somebody who endured great physical suffering may say, "I went through hell in that experience." But those kinds of statements must be understood as hyperbole—that is, as obvious exaggeration. If we could locate the most miserable person alive in the world today, someone who is experiencing suffering at the worst possible level in this world, that person still derives certain benefits from the presence of God. This is because God's graciousness and love of benevolence (what we call His common grace) that He gives to all people are not totally removed from any individual during this lifetime. But in hell, this grace is totally removed. To be in a place where the blessings and the grace of God are utterly and completely absent would be far worse than anything we could possibly imagine that could befall us in this world. So I do not take a whole lot of comfort in thinking that hell is the absence of God.

Hell is the absence of God's benefits; it's the absence of God's love of benevolence. I think that if the people in hell could take a vote or have a referendum to deport one person from their midst—that is, to expel one person from hell—the universal vote would be given to God, because the person who is most unwelcome in hell is God Himself. It would be wonderful for the people in hell if God deserted them altogether.

The problem with hell is not simply the absence of God in terms of the absence of His graciousness. It is the presence of God that is so difficult, because in hell God is present, since He is omnipresent. As the psalmist declares: "Where shall I go from your Spirit? Or where shall I flee from your presence? If I ascend to heaven, you are there! If I make my bed in Sheol, you are there!" (Ps. 139:7–8). If God is everywhere in His being, then certainly He is in hell as much as He is anywhere else. The problem is what He is doing there. He's there in His judgment. He is there in His punitive wrath. He is present in hell as the One who executes His justice on those who are there. That is why I say that anyone in hell would want God, more than anyone else, to leave, because this is our fundamental nature as sinners: to be fugitives from the presence of God. The very first sin evoked the response in Adam and Eve of fleeing from God's presence and hiding from Him. The last thing they wanted after they experienced guilt and shame was for God to be present, and that, if you can multiply it infinitely, is the experience of those who are in hell.

Jesus says that this is the place of "outer darkness" (Matt. 25:30). To understand the force of that, we have to think of it in light of the Old Testament imagery about the outer places and the outer darkness. For the Jews, God described two alternatives to those who received His law. To those who would keep the law, He promised blessedness; for those who renounced or rejected or disobeyed His law, they were to be visited with the curse of God. The whole concept of curse, in the Old Testament, was articulated within the imagery of darkness and of an outer darkness. This was the darkness that was outside the commonwealth of Israel, outside the camp. It was the darkness that came upon Jerusalem when Christ went to the cross. Conversely, the presence of God was described as a place of light, where the glory of God radiated all around. When Jesus warns about the outer darkness, He's warning about the place of the curse, the place where the light and radiance of God's countenance do not shine.

Jesus also said that in this place "there will be weeping and gnashing of teeth" (Matt. 25:30). Again, this is a concrete image that any Jew would understand, and I think we can all readily understand. There are different kinds of weeping. There's the weeping of those who mourn. There's the weeping of those who are in pain. There's the weeping of those who are deliriously happy. But when we add to this notion of weeping a "gnashing of teeth," it is obvious that Jesus is not describing a pleasant circumstance. Jesus is talking about a deep, mournful kind of wailing. And yet when we examine the image of the gnashing of teeth in the New Testament, we find that it is most often associated with hatred. For example, after the crowd heard Stephen proclaim the Word of God, they gnashed their teeth in fury (see Acts 7:54). We should understand that when people are in hell, they are not improving their relationship to God. A person goes to hell in the first place because that person is hostile toward God. When God sends people into the outer darkness where they weep in pain, they also gnash their teeth in even greater hatred of their Maker.

Chapter Seven

The Great Separation

As we continue with our study of the biblical concept of hell, we turn again to Matthew's gospel:

"When the Son of Man comes in his glory, and all the angels with him, then he will sit on his glorious throne. Before him will be gathered all the nations, and he will separate people one from another as a shepherd separates the sheep from the goats. And he will place the sheep on his right, but the goats on the left. Then the King will say to those on his right, 'Come, you who are blessed by my Father, inherit the kingdom prepared for you from the foundation of the world. For I was hungry and you gave me food, I was thirsty and you gave me drink, I was a stranger and you welcomed me, I was naked and you clothed me, I was sick and you visited me, I was in prison and you came to me.' Then the righteous will answer him, saying, 'Lord, when did we see you hungry and feed you, or thirsty and give you drink? And when did we see you a stranger and welcome you, or naked and clothe you? And when did we see you sick or in prison and visit you?' And the King will answer them, 'Truly, I say to you, as you did it to one of the least of these my brothers, you did it to me.'

"Then he will say to those on his left, 'Depart from me, you cursed, into the eternal fire prepared for the devil and his angels. For I was hungry and you gave me no food, I was thirsty and you gave me no drink, I was a stranger and you did not welcome me, naked and you did not clothe me, sick and in prison and you did not visit me.'" (Matt. 25:31–43)

Jesus uses an image of separation here. He talks about the King who will separate kingdoms and people as One who divides sheep from goats. The sheep are those who have been obedient, who have been followers of Christ, who will inherit the kingdom of heaven that was prepared for them from the foundation of the world. The goats, on the other hand, will be excluded from the presence of God and His angels in heaven, and they will be sent away into everlasting fire. Jesus is discussing the concept of judgment.

It's interesting that the New Testament word for judgment is the Greek word *krisis*, from which we get the English word *crisis*. It comes directly over into our language from the Greek. But the supreme crisis for humanity will be the crisis of the last judgment. That will be the time of separation.

Behind the New Testament concept of hell stand some other ideas that we must first understand if this idea of hell is going to make sense to us. First, there is the concept of God's justice. We say that God is just and that He judges according to His own holiness and perfect righteousness. Second, God is the government of the universe; He rules over all people. The point here is that God holds every human being personally accountable to Him. Third, if

Jesus Christ taught anything in His earthly ministry, it is that there will be a final judgment for human beings. Every one of us will be called to account before the presence of God, and we will be judged by His perfect righteousness and by His perfect law.

The New Testament imagery of the last judgment includes those who are accused in the tribunal or the courtroom of God. Their response at the last judgment to the charges leveled against them by the perfect and holy God is silence. Every mouth will be stopped because a person can say nothing to defend himself against the Judge who is perfectly just and who is omniscient. There is no reason to try to lie our way through the trial because we know that we can't fool our Creator, who has a perfect record of everything that we have ever done or thought or said. As the Old Testament proclaims about God, "Even before a word is on my tongue, behold, O Lord, you know it altogether" (Ps. 139:4). Jesus warns of this last judgment; on that occasion, every idle word will be brought into the judgment.

That means that God is going to hold us individually accountable not just for everything that we've ever done but for everything that we've ever said. Even the casual remark, even the offhand statement, even the idle words will be brought into the judgment. And if our idle words are going to be brought into the judgment, how much more will those words that we speak with great seriousness come before His judgment?

The author of Hebrews asks: "How shall we escape if we neglect such a great salvation? It was declared at first by the Lord, and it was attested to us by those who heard" (Heb. 2:3). There is no escape. We are warned that "our God is a consuming fire" (12:29). But we don't like to think that we will ever be held accountable for our actions in this world.

The universal assumption in American culture is that if there is life after death, then everybody's going to go to the same place, to the eternal blessedness of heaven. Nothing turns a sinner into a saint faster than death. You can take the most reprobate people, and when we lay them to rest, we speak confidently that they are enjoying felicity at last; they are at peace in heaven. But in fact, they may have just entered the gates of hell. To contemplate their present condition is more than we can humanly bear. One of the reasons that there is such a profound emotional and visceral response to the doctrine of hell is that it's difficult for anybody to contemplate another human being's going there. We cannot enjoy the thought of even a despicable person's being in hell.

What do we do with the emphatic teaching of Christ and of the New Testament that there will be a judgment and a separation? Some people will, indeed, enter heaven, and others will be cast out into that place of outer darkness, where there's weeping and gnashing of teeth.

I think the most terrifying sermon ever preached was the Sermon on the Mount. Jesus pronounces the blessings: Blessed are the poor, and blessed are those who mourn, and blessed are the peacemakers, and so on. He then ends the sermon by warning the people that on the last day many will come to Him, saying, "Lord, Lord, did we not prophesy in your name, and cast out demons in your name, and do many mighty works in your name?" (Matt. 7:22). Jesus goes on, "And then will I declare to them, 'I never knew you; depart from me, you workers of lawlessness'" (v. 23). "I never knew you." Let's just stop for a second and think about that.

Jesus declares that there will be those who will be rejected by Him and by God on the occasion of the last judgment, and that the situation we enter at death will be final. Now is the day of salvation. Nothing in Scripture gives us the slightest hint that there will be a second chance after death. The longer we postpone our repentance and our fleeing to Christ, the more dangerous and perilous is our condition, for tonight our souls may be required of us. We can't assume that everybody is going to walk peaceably into heaven and escape this judgment—not if we're to take Jesus' teaching seriously. He does speak of separation. He speaks of a crisis, and it is the crisis of surviving the judgment of God.

Let's look at the last few verses of Matthew 25: "Then they also will answer, saying, 'Lord, when did we see you hungry or thirsty or a stranger or naked or sick or in prison, and did not minister to you?' Then he will answer them, saying, 'Truly, I say to you, as you did not do it to one of the least of these, you did not do it to me.' And these will go away into eternal punishment, but the righteous into eternal life" (vv. 44–46). Again, Jesus makes it clear that there will be a time of separation. And that separation will be the greatest crisis that anyone can ever face.

In the Bible, the word "to save" is used to describe many different things. If you are restored to health from a threatening illness, your life has been saved; you have experienced salvation. If an army escapes sure defeat in battle, they experience salvation. But when we talk about the doctrine of salvation, we're talking about ultimate salvation.

The fundamental meaning of salvation is to escape from some calamity. So when we speak about ultimate salvation in the Scriptures, we're talking about an escape from the ultimate calamity. And what is that ultimate calamity? It is the wrath of God visited justly upon those who have remained hostile to Him.

That from which we are ultimately saved is God. We like to think of God as the Savior, as the One who redeems us from judgment. Indeed, He is our Savior, if we have genuinely repented and cast ourselves on the mercy of Christ. Yet to be saved is not simply to be saved *by* Him but also to be saved *from* Him, because the ultimate crisis, the worst calamity a person could ever face, is the judgment of a holy God who will judge us in perfect righteousness.

It's not that we're afraid of being brought before a corrupt and unjust judge who might punish us beyond what we deserve. But rather, the fear is being visited by a Judge who is just and who will judge us perfectly according to what we deserve, according to what we have earned, according to our merit. The Bible makes it clear that the only merit we bring to the throne of God in the last judgment is demerit. The only thing we have earned at the hands of perfect justice is perfect punishment.

We're at ease in Zion nowadays. Preachers aren't preaching hell. This message of Christ's has been all but deleted from the New Testament of our day. We say, "We don't have anything to worry about from God because God is so loving that He is going to save everybody." Well, if He is going to save everybody, it will not be without a serious rebuke against His only begotten Son for teaching falsely that there will be separation, that there will be curse as well as blessing, that there will be punishment as well as the gracious rewards that are given, and that hell was created for the devil, his angels, and all who willingly participate with them.

Chapter Eight

Degrees of Punishment

We have to take a deep breath whenever we approach such a terrifying idea as hell. Paul writes: "Therefore you have no excuse, O man, every one of you who judges. For in passing judgment on another you condemn yourself, because you, the judge, practice the very same things. . . . Do you suppose, O man—you who judge those who practice such things and yet do them yourself—that you will escape the judgment of God?" (Rom. 2:1, 3).

Like Jesus, Paul brings in the theme of a just judgment at the hands of God. Paul likewise warns us of fleeing to escape from the wrath that is surely to come. People will say that the idea of hell that has historically been taught in orthodox Christianity demeans the very character of God, that somehow the doctrine of hell casts a shadow over God's goodness. They will protest: "My God is a God of love. And my God is a good God. If God is loving, and if God is good, He would never, ever send anyone to hell." Let's examine the logic of the statement "If God were really loving, there would be no hell."

What if I asserted, "If a parent were really loving, he would never chasten or punish his child"? People might object to that analogy, saying that the punishment that a loving parent gives to a child is corrective. It is a chastisement that is designed to help the child avoid further difficulties later in life. And certainly the New Testament teaches that God chastens those whom He loves but that His chastisement is for a moment (see Heb. 12:6, 11). It is given for our welfare and for our well-being. Yet when we're talking about hell, we're not talking about God's manifestation of what we call, in theology, His corrective wrath, but we are talking about God's manifesting His punitive wrath—that is, the wrath that is designed not simply for moral improvement of those who receive it but as an expression of God's justice. People object, "If God is really loving, how can He then give punitive wrath to people?"

We have to consider what the objective of God's love is. Some think that God loves all people and therefore brings all people to heaven. The Bible does speak of a kind of love that God displays toward all mankind, His love of benevolence, by which He pours out the blessings of creation—things such as sun, rain, and the seasons. This love is unconditional. But this love is not a saving love, and it is not eternal; it lasts only as long as the earth does.

While God's love of benevolence does not save, it has a purpose. In pouring out blessings on people who have not repented and who have not come to faith, He gives people opportunity to repent and to take advantage of the mercy that is offered in Jesus Christ.

In this instance God is loving us as sinful creatures in a benevolent way, but He also has a greater love. And that is the love He has for righteousness and the love He has for His own character. God is not going to negotiate His holiness or righteousness in order to accommodate us and the ways that we fall short of His glory. There is the sense in which God loves His own glory, and the punishment of recalcitrant, impenitent persons in hell redounds to the glory of God.

This may be one of the most difficult concepts for us ever to grasp: that hell, in one sense, glorifies God. Why? How? The first thing it does to glorify God is that it shows forth, in clear terms, the goodness of God. But wait a minute. I just said that the two most frequent objections against hell involve His love and His goodness; if God were really loving—the way He ought to be loving—then there would be no one in hell. Now, if the love of God means that hell must be empty, then it must be that goodness demands that God be loving enough to save everybody regardless of the person's response. In other words, if He is loving and if He is good, no one will ever go to hell. But consider this. Does a good judge, a just judge, leave evil unpunished? Would we say of the courts in this world that if they refuse to bring judgment on those who were known to be guilty of gross and heinous crimes, then they render good verdicts? Would we consider that justice? Of course not.

A theologian friend of mine was serving on a jury, and the foreman of the jury said, "We're not here to discern right and wrong, but to deal with human relationships."

That's the mentality of our age. What God really should care about are human relationships. That should be the central concern—not the punishment of evil. God would not be good if He insisted on punishing wickedness, people say.

Now, I think God would not be good if He didn't punish wickedness. God would not be good if He completely abandoned His own righteousness or His own justice. But we are convinced, or at least we cross our fingers and hope, that God will not be just, that God will not be good. Again, the problem with hell is not the badness of God. The problem is the goodness of God. It's because God is good, because He hates evil, that there is such a place as hell where He punishes evil.

Romans 2:2 says, "We know that the judgment of God rightly falls on those who practice such things." When God executes His judgment, He does so rightly. "Do you suppose, O man—you who judge those who practice such things and yet do them yourself—that you will escape the judgment of God?" (v. 3). Paul is asking a question here: "Do you think, if you are sinning, that you are going to escape the judgment of God?" He gives this teaching in anticipation of his later unfolding the gospel of forgiveness and justification by the free mercy of God. He's laying the foundation for us to understand the cross and the doctrine of justification; he's saying that unless you have a Savior, you're in serious trouble. He's addressing people who think that they don't need Christ, who think that they will escape the judgment of God.

Are you depending on your hope that God is going to be merciful to you in spite of your refusal to embrace His Son? I find no reason anywhere in Scripture to hope that God will be anything but relentless in His insistence that to escape hell, one must repent of his sins and come to Christ. When Paul spoke at Mars Hill to the cultural center of the ancient world and in the presence of the philosophers, he spoke of the long-suffering of God: "The times of ignorance God overlooked, but now he commands all people everywhere to repent, because he has fixed a day on which he will judge the world in righteousness by a man whom he has appointed; and of this he has given assurance to all by raising him from the dead" (Acts 17:30–31). Paul doesn't give repentance as optional. He's not an evangelist who urges, "All you have to do is walk the walk, come down the aisle, raise your hand, or read this prayer after me." The Apostle doesn't invite people to be saved. He commands them. That is, God commands them.

What happens if you disobey this command? Most of the world is doing exactly that, and they think that they will escape the judgment of God. And they can listen to preacher after preacher and to theologian after theologian who will give them all the security they desire. They cry, "Peace, peace!" when there is no peace and will reinforce their hope that God is not going to judge them. And they do it by denying the very reality of hell.

Paul continues in Romans 2:

Or do you presume on the riches of his kindness and forbearance and patience, not knowing that God's kindness is meant to lead you to repentance? But because of your hard and impenitent heart you are storing up wrath for yourself on the day of wrath when God's righteous judgment will be revealed.

He will render to each one according to his works: to those who by patience in well-doing seek for glory and honor and immortality, he will give eternal life; but for those who are self-seeking and do not obey the truth, but obey unrighteousness, there will be wrath and fury. There will be tribulation and distress for every human being who does evil. (Rom. 2:4–9)

That's a scary thing, because what Paul is describing is a hoarder, someone who amasses a supply of something. Paul says here that those who neglect the goodness and the patience and long-suffering of God, who assume that they're going to escape the wrath of His judgment apart from relying on Christ, are storing up wrath against the day of wrath.

I once was in charge of an ordination exam for a man who wanted to be a minister. During that examination, I asked him if he believed in degrees of guilt. He emphatically responded in the negative: "No, everybody's equally guilty. All sin is equally heinous. James says, 'If you sin against one point of the law, you sin against the whole law.'" The man seeking ordination concluded from that text that all sin is equal, and that you either get to heaven or don't get to heaven. There are no different levels in heaven or gradations of felicity there, or levels to hell, as Dante imagined in his famous *Inferno*.

But here, Paul is talking about hoarding judgment, amassing wrath, heaping it up, piling it up. Every time we sin, every day that we delay in repenting of our sin and coming to faith in Christ, we are adding to our guilt before God, adding to our punishment in hell, adding to the judgment of God's perfect justice. Remember, in His perfect justice, He punishes each sin justly. If we're guilty of five counts of murder and somebody else is guilty of only one count of murder, the punishment that God gives in His final courtroom will be perfectly just. Those who have committed five murders will be judged five times more harshly than those who commit only one murder. We don't have the ability to do that in this world, but God does. This is the sober warning of the Apostle, that we are building a case against ourselves. The longer we sin without repentance and without fleeing to Christ, the worse our judgment will be.

Jesus Himself teaches this concept repeatedly in His own lessons. He speaks of the unprofitable steward, and He talks about those who will receive a light beating and those who will receive a severe beating (Luke 12:35–49). He talks about the judgment that will fall on Bethsaida as greater than the judgment that will go to Tyre and Sidon (Matt. 11:20–24). Jesus tells us that to whom much is given, much is required. There will be various degrees of punishment because hell is the place of the exacting of perfect justice. Though we are all guilty and deserve to go to hell, there are degrees and gradations of guilt of those who go there. Just as the rewards in heaven will differ according to the level of obedience we offer to Christ during our lifetime, so the punitive wrath of God in hell will differ in intensity according to one's life and opportunity.

Our problem with hell is twofold. First, we deny it. Second, even if we affirm it or think it might be true, we neutralize it by saying that everybody's in the same boat and that everybody receives the same punishment. Now, I don't want to be in even the highest level of hell. Even given the degrees of reward and felicity in heaven and the degrees of punishment in hell, the gap between either place is almost infinite. It's a huge, unbridgeable chasm, as we will see in the next chapter. We have to understand our peril in taking for granted the mercy of God and in tempting God, assuming that He is incapable of or unwilling to bring us to justice. When we are brought to that tribunal, if we're given the righteousness of Christ for our justification, we will escape His wrath. But if we abandon, avoid, or neglect Christ, then we will be brought only to justice.

Chapter Nine

The Point of No Return

Jesus tells a parable that is significant to any discussion of the concept of hell. It is usually called the parable of the rich man and Lazarus.

"There was a rich man who was clothed in purple and fine linen and who feasted sumptuously every day. And at his gate was laid a poor man named Lazarus, covered with sores, who desired to be fed with what fell from the rich man's table. Moreover, even the dogs came and licked his sores. The poor man died and was carried by the angels to Abraham's side. The rich man also died and was buried, and in Hades, being in torment, he lifted up his eyes and saw Abraham far off and Lazarus at his side." (Luke 16:19–23)

When we study a parable in the New Testament, the general rule of interpretation is that the parable has one central point. This is not always the case; the parable of the sower makes several significant points. But the danger with parables is trying to find a meaning or significance in every individual point. We would get lost in a sea of confusion if we were to do that.

Having said that, I want to add one other thing. When Jesus borrows illustrations from nature or from the common life of the people, or when He tells a fictitious story to illustrate a point, though not every point in the story may carry with it a certain theological message, we can rest assured that Jesus would not make a statement that would be principally incorrect—that is, He would not use as part of His illustration some idea in direct conflict with the teaching of the Word of God that is found elsewhere. So that gives us a bit of license to speculate in principle about some of the secondary ideas that are contained in a parable. With that in mind, let's look at this opening segment of the parable.

He begins by contrasting two human beings. One is fabulously wealthy. The other is living a miserable existence marked not only by abject poverty but also by a relentless suffering, a man who is stricken and afflicted with sores from which the only relief he ever receives comes from dogs that lick them. This man is in a most miserable condition.

The rich man was clothed in purple and fine linen. The ancient person would understand that this was someone who lived the lifestyle of a king, for kings were garbed in purple. Jesus describes this man's riches in the most elegant terms because only those with a fabulous amount of wealth could afford garments that were dyed purple and spun from fine linen. The picture here is one of extreme contrast, between fabulous wealth and fabulous poverty.

This might incline us to think that the main point Jesus is trying to communicate in the parable is that all poor people go to heaven and all rich people go to hell, but we must not draw that conclusion because that would put the parable on a collision course with what the Scriptures teach elsewhere. The Bible records many examples of people who were fabulously wealthy *and* profoundly godly. Abraham was one of the wealthiest men of the ancient world, and he is enjoying the ultimate degree of heaven in this parable. Joseph of Arimathea, another man of great wealth, is noted for having Jesus buried in his tomb. The Bible doesn't say that anybody who is wealthy will go to hell or that it is intrinsically sinful to be wealthy. Jesus does, however, frequently warn of the difficulties of coming into the kingdom of God for those who have vast amounts of resources, for such people have a tendency to think of themselves as self-sufficient. In the parable of the rich fool, the wealthy man was so concerned about amassing wealth in this world that he neglected the care of his own soul (see Luke 12:13–21). But again, Jesus is not teaching a doctrine that all poor people go to heaven. The Bible denies both justification by wealth and justification by poverty. There's no inherent virtue in being poor. So often, however, it is the poor people who flock to the comforts of Christ because they find no comfort in this world, no satisfaction in the things that they have or don't have, and they seem to be more open to hearing the message of the kingdom of God.

We are told in our parable that the rich man fared sumptuously every day. His life was one of uninterrupted pleasure and hedonism. "And at his gate was laid a poor man named Lazarus, covered with sores, who desired to be fed with what fell from the rich man's table" (Luke 16:20–21). This is not the only time the Bible speaks of those who seek to be fed from others' leftovers. The Old Testament allowed for gleaning, meaning that landowners and farmers were not to harvest and sell everything that they produced. Rather, they were to leave the corners of their fields open for the poor to pick up what was left over from the harvest so that they would not be utterly destitute. You may see people today who, in a pathetic expression of poverty, walk around with a bag that contains everything that they own, or they may even be pushing a cart in which all their earthly goods are contained. They may go from one refuse container to another, looking for scraps of food that people have thrown away. So it was with this beggar, Lazarus, who lay at the gate, hoping to sustain himself from the garbage of the wealthy man.

Then we are told, "The poor man died and was carried by the angels to Abraham's side" (v. 22). Now, again, we have to be careful here. Is Jesus teaching that anytime a saint dies and goes to heaven, he is borne into the presence of God by these angelic messengers, or is this part of the imagery He uses to describe the great beauty of the afterlife? I don't know the answer to that question, but it's fun to speculate a little bit, isn't it? It certainly doesn't violate any principle of Scripture to think that at the moment we die, we meet an escort, and that the escort or escorts are the angels who carry us into the presence of Christ. Wouldn't it be remarkable if, at the moment we ceased this life, we were immediately in the presence of the angels? Think of the spiritual "Swing Low, Sweet Chariot": "I looked over Jordan, and what did I see, comin' for to carry me home? A band of angels comin' after me, comin' for to carry me home." Those lines are taken right from this text. We find a biblical precedent for this idea in the Old Testament when the prophet Elijah is taken up to heaven in a whirlwind (see 2 Kings 2). That indicates the presence of the shekinah glory, the presence of the glory that is mediated by the angels. I like to think that this is normative—that is, that Jesus is adding a detail here that is borrowed from the full content of biblical revelation and that we, as His people, can look forward to the same kind of escort service that transcends any liveried limousine we might enjoy in this world.

Jesus calls the place to which the beggar is taken by the angels "Abraham's side." This phrase is sometimes translated "Abraham's bosom," which is sometimes used as an indirect name for heaven, the place where the father of the faithful is now resting in his eternal felicity. Then we're told that "the rich man also died and was buried, and in Hades, being in torment, he lifted up his eyes and saw Abraham far off and Lazarus at his side" (Luke 16:22–23). Now, this does not necessarily mean that people who are in hell have the ability to see people who are in heaven, and vice versa. But because Jesus draws this picture, it's hard to resist the inference that this indeed may be the case. At least for the purposes of His parable, Jesus describes the rich man's ability, in the midst of his awful, dreadful torment, to see the splendor and joy that he is missing and that the poor man is enjoying.

Then we read, "And he called out, 'Father Abraham, have mercy on me, and send Lazarus to dip the end of his finger in water and cool my tongue, for I am in anguish in this flame'" (v. 24). This does not necessarily mean that hell is a local place of fire, as we've already indicated, and that the torment is one of intense heat. But the point Jesus is making here is that the sinner in hell would give everything he had and do anything he could do to make the number of sins that he had committed in this world one less. The rich sinner is seeking some relief from the pain, and now he's begging for help from the beggar he ignored. He's not asking for a sumptuous dinner to be sent down from heaven. All he asks is that Lazarus would dip the tip of his finger in the cool water and come and touch his tongue. "Give me the slightest bit of relief" is the cry of the rich man. It's also interesting that he makes this cry with the words "have mercy on me." I wonder whether, by this point, the man understands that the torment he's suffering is just and that if any balm were given to his pain, it would be an act of mercy.

> "But Abraham said, 'Child, remember that you in your lifetime received your good things, and Lazarus in like manner bad things; but now he is comforted here, and you are in anguish. And besides all this, between us and you a great chasm has been fixed, in order that those who would pass from here to you may not be able, and none may cross from there to us.' And he said, 'Then I beg you, father, to send him to my father's house—for I have five brothers—so

that he may warn them, lest they also come into this place of torment.' But Abraham said, 'They have Moses and the Prophets; let them hear them.' And he said, 'No, father Abraham, but if someone goes to them from the dead, they will repent.' He said to him, 'If they do not hear Moses and the Prophets, neither will they be convinced if someone should rise from the dead.'" (vv. 25–31)

We know that we live in a topsy-turvy world where, as one poet said, "princes walk in rags and beggars ride on horses" (see Eccl. 10:7). The wicked prosper and the righteous suffer. But that will be turned around in the ultimate kingdom of God, for God will vindicate those who have been oppressed and unjustly wounded in this world. Retribution will set the scales of justice in an even manner. We also notice that in his plea, the rich man begs Abraham to send Lazarus to warn his brothers, lest they fall into the same misery.

I think the principal point of the parable is this: A great gulf is fixed between heaven and hell. Once a person lives his life here, there is no bridge from hell to heaven after death. As the Bible says, we live our lives, we die, and we are appointed for the judgment. There is no second chance beyond the grave. Jesus tells us, through the lips of Abraham, that how we die is final for all of us.

Perhaps one of the greatest follies we find ourselves committing is the folly of procrastination. We keep saying to ourselves that tomorrow we're going to turn over a new leaf, tomorrow we will make ourselves right with God, but right now we're not quite ready. That was the song of the rich fool, and his foolishness was shown in the warning: "Fool! This night your soul is required of you" (Luke 12:20). We are not to postpone our redemption by such procrastination. "Behold, now," the Scriptures tell us, again and again, "is the day of salvation" (2 Cor. 6:2). The rich man in hell pleads, "Then I beg you, father, to send [Lazarus] to my father's house—for I have five brothers—so that he may warn them, lest they also come into this place of torment" (Luke 16:27–28). And the answer is this: "They have Moses and the Prophets; let them hear them" (v. 29). If they haven't listened to Moses and the Prophets, what made the rich man think they would listen to Lazarus? Indeed, Jesus asserts that they wouldn't even listen to one who is raised from the dead (see v. 31). Beloved, Christ has come back from the grave.

And yet we do not listen to Him. We have the opportunity now, today, to hear Him, to flee to Him, and to embrace Him. Today may, indeed, be the last opportunity you will ever have.

About the Author

Dr. R.C. Sproul was the founder of Ligonier Ministries, founding pastor of Saint Andrew's Chapel in Sanford, Fla., first president of Reformation Bible College, and executive editor of *Tabletalk* magazine. His radio program, *Renewing Your Mind*, is still broadcast daily on hundreds of radio stations around the world and can also be heard online. He was the author of more than one hundred books, including *The Holiness of God*, *Chosen by God*, and *Everyone's a Theologian*. He was recognized throughout the world for his articulate defense of the inerrancy of Scripture and the need for God's people to stand with conviction upon His Word.

Free eBooks *by* R.C. Sproul

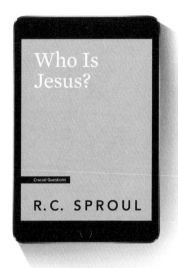

Does prayer really change things? Can I be sure I'm saved? Dr. R.C. Sproul answers these important questions, along with more than forty others, in his Crucial Questions series. Designed for the Christian or thoughtful inquirer, these booklets can be used for personal study, small groups, and conversations with family and friends. Browse the collection and download your free digital ebooks today.

 Ligonier.org/freeCQ

Get 3 free months
of *Tabletalk*.

In 1977, R.C. Sproul started *Tabletalk* magazine.
Today it has become the most widely read subscriber-based monthly
devotional magazine in the world. **Try it free for 3 months.**

𝕋 TryTabletalk.com/CQ | 800-435-4343

ASK LIGONIER

Do we have free will?

Is it true that God controls everything?

Does prayer change things?

A Place to Find Answers

Maybe you're leading a Bible study tomorrow. Maybe you're just beginning to dig deeper. It's good to know that you can always ask Ligonier. For more than fifty years, Christians have been looking to Ligonier Ministries, the teaching fellowship of R.C. Sproul, for clear and helpful answers to biblical and theological questions. Now you can ask those questions online as they arise, confident that our team will work quickly to provide clear, concise, and trustworthy answers. The *Ask Ligonier* podcast provides another avenue for you to submit questions to some of the most trusted pastors and teachers who are serving the church today. When you have questions, just ask Ligonier.

FOR MORE INFORMATION, VISIT ASK.LIGONIER.ORG